An Invitation to
PRAY & WORSHIP
JOURNEY TO A DEEPER FAITH

John Tesh

with Wendy Lee Nentwig

COUNTRYMAN

NASHVILLE, TENNESSEE

"*As Christians, worship and prayer are two of the most powerful weapons we have.*"

—JOHN TESH

Discovering the power we have

through prayer and worship

has changed my life.

DISCOVER THE POWER

Whenever anything makes a huge impact on your life, you get this excitement about sharing it with others. That's what this book is about.

I grew up going to church three times a week. My dad was in charge of the Sunday school program, and my mom was head of the women's auxiliary. One of my uncles is a Baptist preacher to this day. I had everything memorized.

And then I got to college. I took a course where I was taught that religion is nothing more than an explanation for things you don't really understand; it's just a crutch.

At that same time, the Vietnam War was raging, everything seemed turned upside down, and I was a mess. I didn't really believe in anything except whatever was going to make me feel good. Eventually, I married, but it was for the wrong reasons and it fell apart. My life was going to pieces.

A year later, I ran into a woman named Concetta (Connie) who seemed very much together. She started introducing me to people and presenting me with challenges that would change my life. That was twelve years ago.

I've learned a lot during that time about prayer and worship. Much of it has come from Louis, our pastor, and from the small–but–vibrant congregation where I lead worship each week. I don't have all the answers and, like you, I'm still on this journey. But discovering the power we have through prayer and worship has changed my life. I hope it can do the same for you.

—JOHN TESH

THE POWER OF Prayer

"WHEN YOU PRAY, DON'T BE LIKE THOSE PEOPLE WHO DON'T KNOW GOD.

THEY CONTINUE SAYING THINGS THAT MEAN NOTHING, THINKING THAT

GOD WILL HEAR THEM BECAUSE OF THEIR MANY WORDS. DON'T BE LIKE

THEM, BECAUSE YOUR FATHER KNOWS THE THINGS YOU NEED BEFORE

YOU ASK HIM."

—MATTHEW 6:7–8

THE PERVASIVENESS OF PRAYER

MY DAUGHTER, PRIMA, ASKS ME ALL THE TIME, "How can God hear every single prayer? How does that happen?" I have to admit I don't have a satisfactory answer for her. I can't explain all the intricacies of prayer, I only know that it works. You only have to look at my life—at all the mistakes I've made and how it's turned out—to know the only explanation is prayer.

That's the one thing I never lost in my life. When I wasn't going to church, when I was living in sin, the one constant I had was prayer. I can never remember not praying.

THE MOST DANGEROUS PRAYER

THE MOST POWERFUL PRAYER YOU CAN PRAY ALSO HAPPENS TO BE THE MOST dangerous one. That prayer was given to me by my friend and Christian therapist Dr. Steven Brigham. That prayer is "God, do whatever it takes to bring me deeper into Your kingdom." Pray it every day consistently, and I guarantee that your life will change, but probably not the way you expect it to. It is, indeed, the most dangerous prayer.

WHEN PROGRESS IS ANYTHING BUT

MODERN ADVANCES ARE GREAT, BUT THEY don't necessarily make it easier to stay in tune with God. Email alone has changed the way we make decisions. As a result of that readily available "Send" key, we now make about ninety percent of our decisions without praying about them. We sit at our computers sending out reply after reply, when what God really wants is for us to sit and be still and listen and ask. Our "high-speed connection" leaves us fully disconnected. The information superhighway has led to a lot of really bad decisions. We're all day–trading our lives away.

"Pray continually."

—1 THESSALONIANS 5:17

MY PASTOR PREACHED A GREAT MESSAGE RECENTLY ABOUT PRAYER. HE'S ALWAYS being asked, "When is the best time to pray? Should I go in the closet in the morning? Sit down with a prayer journal in the evening?" So he came up with a solution.

In this day and age when we're all on the phone endlessly, he advises people to think of your conversation with God as being the first call you receive each morning. When you wake up, you are connected for the day. The lines of prayer communication are open. Then when something else comes along to distract you—another call or a business meeting or an errand—that's call waiting. Take that call and give it your attention for the necessary amount of time, but when you're done, don't forget to click back over to that conversation with God.

That is the metaphor I use for my prayer life right now. I always try to be connected—and I admit it's not easy to do—but God wants us to stay plugged in . . . online. He's our lifeline.

God is our lifeline.

"One of our biggest misconceptions

about prayer is that it's difficult."

—JOHN TESH

THE NUMBER ONE FEAR OF PEOPLE ALL ACROSS THE UNITED STATES IS not death, poverty or dismemberment . . . it's public speaking. We are terrified of being embarrassed and judged at the hands of other humans. I believe we carry that crippling fear over into prayer. We're so afraid that we're going to pray and not get it right. That we're going to come off like a "Monty Python" skit. As a result we end up not praying at all. But I've talked to dozens of Christian leaders and they all say the same thing: Prayer isn't a public address, it's a personal conversation. All you have to do is talk. God's just waiting to listen.

Prayer isn't a public address, it's a personal conversation.

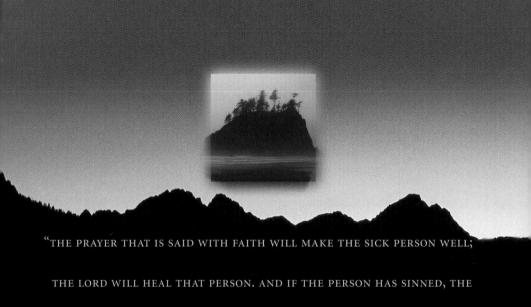

"THE PRAYER THAT IS SAID WITH FAITH WILL MAKE THE SICK PERSON WELL;

THE LORD WILL HEAL THAT PERSON. AND IF THE PERSON HAS SINNED, THE

SINS WILL BE FORGIVEN."

—JAMES 5:15

"Prayer makes you more vigilant."

—JOHN TESH

STAYING PHYSICALLY AND SPIRITUALLY FIT

YOU MIGHT LAUGH, BUT MY DEEPEST PRAYER TIME IS WHEN I'm jumping rope. It sounds ridiculous, but for thirty minutes each morning, as the sun is rising, I'm totally focused in this temple of "badump, badump, badump," and that's my prayer time. "O Lord God, forgive me of my sins. O Lord, bless me. Lord Jesus, protect my family, grant me Your mercy." Badump, badump, badump.

A lot of people say, "Oh no. I read where you have to have this special place and your Bible has to be on the table and you have to keep a journal." But that might not work for you, so God gives you permission to find something that does.

After all, God doesn't care where we meet Him, only that we do it.

God doesn't care where we meet Him,

only that we do it.

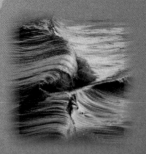

THE TIMES WHEN I HAVEN'T GIVEN THINGS UP

to God in prayer and instead said, "I'm just going to go ahead and make this decision because it feels right," nine times out of ten I've been wrong. God is our Father and our connection to Him through prayer is our board of directors . . . our accountability.

A LOT OF US FEEL AFRAID TO ASK FOR GOD'S blessing. We don't feel worthy. I often tell people God wants to *know* that you want His blessing. You don't have to earn it.

I tell that to other people, but it's always been a big hurdle for me. There are so many times when I don't feel worthy enough to "bother" God with all my wants and needs. I admit I still don't fully understand God's incomprehensible gift of grace.

YOUR MOST IMPORTANT JOB

WE'RE ALWAYS LOOKING FOR SHORTCUTS, BUT THERE'S JUST no way around prayer. I was reminded of that as I watched my daughter struggle to learn the recorder. She would play a few notes and then she'd mess up and start screaming, insisting, "I'm never gonna learn it!"

I assured her she would eventually master this instrument, but that it would take a lot of practice and commitment. There was no way around doing what she was doing. Then I told her, "I'm going to sit here and go through every page with you. I won't leave you. We'll do it together, but you have to do it to learn. There's no way out."

That's how it is with prayer. There's no way out. It's part of your job as a human being if you want to stay connected to God. After all, what's the alternative?

I DON'T EVER LET MY GIRLS——MY WIFE AND MY DAUGHTER

——get out of the house before I lay my hands on them

every morning and pray for their protection, for direction,

and for everything that comes out of our mouths to be

honoring to God. I pray that before we leave our home we

would realize that everything we do and everything

we say has the power to touch somebody.

"Devote yourselves to prayer,

being watchful and thankful."

—COLOSSIANS 4:2 (NIV)

PRAYER WORKS EVERYWHERE, IN EVERY SITUATION.

I'm so convinced of the power of prayer, I've even started asking waiters and waitresses if there's anything I can pray about for them.

I first saw a friend do this, and the waitress burst into tears and fell into his arms. It turns out her boyfriend was dying. So now I ask that regularly, and I've never been turned down. It can be embarrassing at first. I've had people who say "no" initially, but they always come back later and say, "You know, I was just thinking and I *do* have something."

I PRAY FOR BOLDNESS EVERY DAY. I HAVE LEARNED

it's something I really need because we will miss every

important opportunity—whether it's to get deeper

with God or to evangelize—if we don't have boldness.

Prayer works everywhere, in every situation.

Prayer connects us to the life we should be living.

I ONCE DID A RADIO SHOW SEGMENT CALLED "PRAYER 101" WHERE I INTERVIEWED all these amazing people—from Thelma Wells and Bishop Wellington Boone to Steve Arterburn and Gary Smalley. It was almost like having a press conference featuring all the top thinkers about prayer. The funny thing is I interviewed them all at different times, but they all said the same thing. There are so many people out there saying, "How do I pray? When do I pray? Where do I pray?" And they all said, "You just need to do it."

I think that discipline of staying in touch makes you more disciplined in other areas of your life. Even beyond what's happening spiritually, it focuses your moral compass and gives you a passion for a life worth living. We're all looking for a way to live our lives. And when you come to the realization that the way Christ lived His life is the right way, then you say, "I'm going to spend the rest of my life trying to get close to that . . . to emulate that."

I even asked my pastor once if he ever thought, "What if we're wrong?" He said, "Yeah, what if this thing is all a big hoax? But the way I look at it . . . if I am wrong, what an amazing life I tried to live."

Prayer connects us to the life we should be living and it tears us away from the here and now.

THE POWER OF *Worship*

"I WILL PRAISE YOU, LORD, AMONG THE NATIONS.

I WILL SING PRAISES TO YOUR NAME."

—2 SAMUEL 22:50

WORSHIP MUSIC IS USEFUL

WHAT I LOVE ABOUT WORSHIP MUSIC IS THAT IT SPEAKS to people. Eventually, the power of those words and those melodies is going get to you. And during the recording process I can't help feeling like a missionary. I just know that one of those songs is going to minister to somebody. One of those songs is going to change someone's life. It's going to heal a marriage, it's going to be played in a wedding somewhere, it's going to give someone hope who is sick. Worship music is useful.

Hope . . . Healing . . . Change

A NEW WAY TO WORSHIP

MORE THAN A DECADE AGO NOW, GARY SMALLEY INTRODUCED MY family to a camp (Kanakuk) where we ended up sending our son, Gib. He went there and it changed his life. He's twenty–one now, but for the past eleven summers, I've been going there with him and playing in the worship band with these kids.

Now you need to understand, I'm talking about 250 kids in a gym, sweating and worshiping harder than you can imagine.

I grew up in the Westbury Methodist Church on Long Island, New York, where I played organ and trumpet. I was used to all those straight–ahead, classic hymns, which are wonderful, but this was something brand new. So when I heard this music more than ten years ago, songs like "Shout to the Lord," "Trading My Sorrows" and others, they were like nothing I'd ever heard . . . appealing on so many levels and crossing cultural and age barriers. To say they made quite an impact would be an understatement.

AN OFFER I COULDN'T REFUSE

I WASN'T LOOKING FOR MORE ACTIVITIES TO ADD TO MY ALREADY FULL SCHEDULE, but I couldn't help noticing how modern praise songs were really changing the way people were looking at worship. So after I returned from camp one year, I went to the pastor of the small congregation I've attended for years and said, "You and your little worship group need to do this."

He listened and said, "that's fine, but we need you to take the expertise you have working with a band on the road and come be a part of the worship band."

I was playing sixty concerts a year, performing mostly original instrumental music, and so I replied, "I have so much in my life right now. We have a young daughter. I'm running a record company . . . I just can't make that commitment."

The world has us under a magnifying glass.

Louis kept pressuring me in his own way and I finally gave in, but I asked if it would be appropriate to set some ground rules: "We need the musicians to show up on time, and they're going to learn the songs, and they must behave like professionals or they're not going to play." Two or three people left the worship band after dealing with the new guidelines, but I felt it was important to hold what we were doing to a higher standard. I knew people were going to come to our little church and it might be the first time they ever heard these songs. If we were out of tune or off time or playing sloppy arrangements, people were going to say, "What is this? Oh, it's Christian stuff."

The world has us under a magnifying glass. As a result, everything we do has to be that much better. God calls on us to live with excellence.

Everything we do has to be that much better

"Come, let's worship him and bow down.

Let's kneel before the Lord who made us."

—PSALM 95:6

AS WE CONTINUED TO GROW AS A WORSHIP BAND AND TO WRITE some of our own songs, Pastor Louis started saying, "Look at the reaction you're getting! You need to make a record."

My first response was, "I'm concerned about the reaction from fans. I'm not known as a Christian recording artist." But he encouraged me not to think of it that way. "Ask yourself, John, 'where's your heart?'" It was a typical Louis Lapides challenge.

That's really where *A Deeper Faith*, the record we released in 2002, came from. And it allowed us to take worship music where it hadn't been before. We took it to *Regis & Kelly* and to *Larry King*. We went on Fox News and the Home Shopping Network. We even played worship songs at The Mirage in Las Vegas, where people stood on their seats worshiping.

Suddenly this gift from God was allowing me to be useful. I was enjoying this experience sharing salt and light.

Ask yourself, 'where's your heart?'

OUR LITTLE WORSHIP BAND NOW DRAWS PEOPLE FROM ALL OVER the San Fernando Valley, and it's taught me a lot about the power of worship. It's the single most important thing you can offer in a church today because so many people aren't ready to sit through a sermon right away. But if you create the right environment for people to be touched by powerful words and melodies, it is a life–changing experience.

Now, there are times when I just get so completely lost in the music. As I'm leading, I often close my eyes and forget where I am in the song . . . I lose myself. I lose my place in the building, my place on the earth. It's a chilling experience that I am hooked on

LET THE WORSHIP TESTIFY

WORSHIP MUSIC ALLOWS ME TO COMMUNICATE A message of faith to my audience without preaching. Some people may say I need to be more forceful in my Christian message, but I think a lot of folks would rather sing along, get on their chairs and stomp their feet, and become involved in worship than hear about my testimony. I can give my testimony in a church, but a lot of people hurting out there need the message of Jesus in a more gentle, winsome way. Worship music allows me to do that.

"I love standing on stage knowing there's somebody out there who needs to hear what these songs are saying."

—John Tesh

ONE OF THE GREATEST EXPERIENCES I'VE EVER HAD WAS WHEN MY PUBLICIST called me up right after 9/11 and said, "You're going to Africa." I wasn't so sure about going, but she told me that the biggest worship service ever held was

scheduled to take place there. There would be no money and I'd have to pay my own way, but a million people a night would be worshiping harder than I'd ever seen in my life as they prayed for the victims and families and firemen of the September 11, 2001, attacks.

So I found myself on a plane to Nigeria. Some of the people there had never even seen a white person before, and yet they were praying for the hurting people in a country whose ways they couldn't comprehend. And the worshipers owned absolutely nothing by American standards. All they had was their faith. So to see them on their knees, screaming like the Psalmist, shouting to the Lord for protection, for salvation and forgiveness, stomping and clawing at the ground and inviting the Holy Spirit into their hearts, it's just not the way it happens here in America.

As I was riding back to the hotel, I asked the cab driver, "Why would all these people come into this field and stay there all day, many without food or much water, and worship? Why is your faith so deep?"

He pulled the cab over and turned to look me in the eye. "Because we don't have your distractions," he replied. "Here, it's not about the church, it's not about the pastor, it's about the Christ."

When your faith is all you're hanging on to, it becomes the strongest thing you have. I spent a week after that experience being totally and completely ashamed. That's when I really began to understand the power of prayer and worship.

*It's not about the church,
it's not about the pastor,
it's about the Christ.*

I SEE WORSHIP AS BEING SAFE. AS SOON AS

we leave the womb, from that moment on we

are desperate to have arms wrapped around

us again. That, to me, is what worship is. You

end up with an amazing bear hug from God.

That's why I take it so seriously.

"SPEAK TO EACH OTHER WITH PSALMS, HYMNS, AND SPIRITUAL SONGS,

SINGING AND MAKING MUSIC IN YOUR HEARTS TO THE LORD."

—EPHESIANS 5:19

FINDING MY VOICE

UP UNTIL *A DEEPER FAITH* I NEVER REALLY SANG ON ANY OF MY RECORDINGS because I never thought of myself as a singer. So why did I suddenly start singing on a worship CD? It's because it felt ridiculous to be playing piano in the middle of worship service and not singing along. Worship demands full participation.

Worship demands full participation.

WHAT WOULD YOU DO DIFFERENTLY?

I'VE NEVER BEEN SAFE.

I read recently about interviews conducted with people over the age of ninety who were asked all those questions about life that you and I want answered. The final question was, "If you could change anything, what would it be?" The overwhelming response was, "I would risk more."

You can apply that to anything. You could say, "I would risk being honest about my faith" or "I would risk praying more," "I would risk becoming closer to my family." Maybe you'd say, "I would give more of my money away." When I left my job as a co-host on *Entertainment Tonight*, people saw that as a huge risk, but I didn't.

In the same way, I couldn't just play it safe and stick to instrumental music and do public television specials for the rest of my life. I came to a place where I determined never to do anything again that isn't useful on some level. That's why I love playing worship music, because every time you play a worship song on TV or on a radio show, someone is going to be touched. It's not going to have an adverse effect on someone. It can't!

Risk more . . . . worship more.

ONE OF WORSHIP'S BIGGEST STRENGTHS IS ITS ABILITY TO GO PLACES A SERMON can't. In sharing my faith during public appearances, what I've learned after making some mistakes is to wait to be asked. There will never be a shortage of opportunities.

So if I'm on *Live With Regis & Kelly*, I don't start performing "it's all about You . . . all about You, Jesus," because that's going to turn people off. They're not going to understand and may well be offended. Instead, I'll choose a more universal praise song like "I Could Sing of Your Love Forever." (I call it the "pronoun song.") Then when the host asks about the inspiration for the album, I need to be found ready and say, "It's because of my strong belief in Christ that I've been able to have a positive and amazing direction for my family . . . for my life . . . and for my music." Someone observes you . . . they ask you a question . . . you answer it.

As Christians, we often offer our very strong opinions before we're asked by the world. We get pushy with our beliefs. Instead, I try to do what my wife does so well—live my faith and be ready when opportunities fall into place everywhere

ACTIONS SPEAK LOUDER THAN WORDS

USUALLY, WHAT WE DO HAS SO MUCH MORE IMPACT on people than what we say. All my talk about the importance of worship doesn't compare to the actual act. Or as my pastor's wife has made me see, people come to the church and see this guy who has a music career, he's been on public television, he's done all these giant specials . . . and he's playing in this little worship band for free every Sunday. According to her, that act really speaks to people.

What they don't realize is that I can't wait for the week to be over so I can get back in that band. I guarantee you it's more of a blessing for me than for anyone else in the congregation. It's that same feeling that you get when you walk out of the best movie you've ever seen; you can't wait to tell your friends about it. That's the feeling of having been to a great worship service. First, you want to find a way to change your life. Second, you want to tell everyone how you did it.

Great worship

Change your life

Tell everyone.

You're invited to experience
A Deeper Faith.

 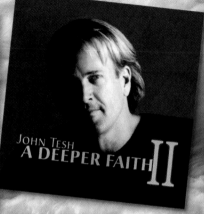

John Tesh's worship celebrations *A Deeper Faith* and *A Deeper Faith 2* are available on CD from Garden City Music. These albums include several of the songs mentioned in this book, and they feature John on lead vocals, as well as on the grand piano.

Available wherever music is sold.

For more information, visit www.tesh.com.